Response From Thought Leaders

"With a combined 60 years of experience, Todd Sipe and Greg Linz have put together a practical and meaningful book that will help you navigate your personal finances based upon the teachings of Jesus. Not only will you gain clarity regarding your finances, you will establish your *Financial Purpose*."

Larry Julian
Author of God is my CEO

"The more I study wealth and money, the more I'm convinced it's a wonderful blessing of a loving Father God and a spiritually powerful but dangerous thing when not used properly. Being clear about its purpose and power in your life is a great and worthwhile investment of time. Building your framework is the beginning of the journey to find your *Financial Purpose*."

Brad Hewitt
Former President and CEO, Thrivent Financial
Author of Your New Money Mindset

"This book not only identifies an enormously important framework for having life-giving *Financial Purpose* but will guide that framework into transformational reality for those who follow its wisdom. Being trustworthy with earthly riches opens up the entire realm of true riches which the Lord intends for each of us."

Jay Bennett
Chair, National Christian Foundation

"I heard a consultant say sometime ago that our brains want to move from confusion to clarity and in order to do that we have to listen to words and concepts that are simple, relevant, and repeatable. Todd and Greg have written a book based upon Scripture that shows that managing one's finances is simple. It's relevant and highly repeatable, which is so important for clarity of communication. I have spent my professional life helping people integrate biblical wisdom with professional knowledge, and I believe this book adds to the body of knowledge that is needed in our complex and confusing world. I recommended it highly and know that many lives will be impacted if they take seriously what is written herein."

Ron Blue
Founder, Kingdom Advisor and Blue Trust
Speaker and author of books including Master Your Money and many more

Packed With Digital Resources

FPpathway.org was created to support your upcoming journey. All exercises in this book are supported by the digital resources on the website. Want to go deeper? Additional resources have been added on many related financial topics.

CREATE YOUR ACCOUNT

1. Go to **https://www.fppathway.org/signup**

2. Create your account. Select **'Log In'** and **'Need an account?'** Provide your email address and create your own password.

3. Enter the Book Activation Code: **MYFRAMEWORK**

4. Explore and enjoy!

A FRAMEWORK FOR LIVING
THE LIFE GOD INTENDED

FINANCIAL
PURPOSE

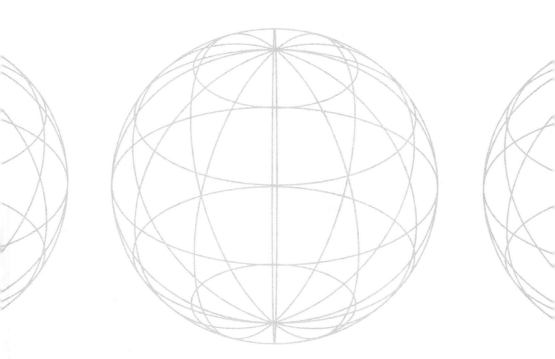

TODD SIPE
& GREG LINZ

Financial Purpose presents a financial framework to help manage spending, savings, debt and giving. The framework is very customizable resulting in a unique pathway for each person. As such, Financial Purpose does not promise outcomes as all responsibility and results are directly on the user to determine and follow their own path. Financial Purpose does not provide investment advice. Please see your Financial Planner. Financial Purpose does not provide tax advice. Please see your Tax Preparer.

All stories is this book are real, although names and personal details may be changed to protect the privacy of those involved.

Cover and images by Ben Burton

Contents

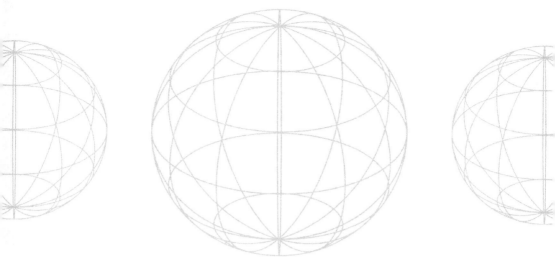

Introduction

*But seek first his kingdom and his righteousness,
and all these things will be given to you as well.*

Matthew 6:33

She couldn't seem to get her head above water.

Kathy was a single mom of three small children who was working three part-time jobs to try to provide for her family. With limited income, no health insurance, and a dependence on government support, financial health didn't seem like it was in the cards for her. You've heard of living paycheck to paycheck? Kathy *dreamed* of living paycheck to paycheck. Instead, she watched the financial hole she was in grow deeper and deeper. Strapped with over $10,000 in credit card debt, her future looked bleak at best.

After years of struggling financially, Kathy realized she needed some help. She found a personal banker and financial team who worked tirelessly with her to create a plan for her finances. The framework they developed would allow her to not only live paycheck to paycheck, but to pay off her debt and even build up a savings reserve of $10,000 in just two years. It wasn't going to be easy, but they had created a pathway to give Kathy a whole new life.

Then reality sank in.

Although the plan they developed could lead to success, it was going to take hard work. Positive changes in our life usually demand sacrifice. Her plan included unhooking from cable TV and modifying her unlimited family cell phone plan. These can certainly be tough choices, but seeing her family make a dramatic leap forward financially made this a no-brainer. But Kathy's response to the recommendations illustrates the power culture has on us. She told her banker if she got rid of cable TV and changed her cell phone plan, she would be considered poor in her neighborhood. Her banker wanted to reply, "Would you rather be considered poor, or actually be poor?" Kathy never realized financial transformation.

If we're honest, culture often wins. Our consumption mindset prioritizes instant gratification at the expense of long-term stability. It's much easier and more fun in the moment to just say yes to that new TV, car, or clothes. With one swipe of a credit card, we can immediately get the rush of that new purchase. But we all know where that leaves us.

While Kathy's story may seem like an extreme case, the dilemma she faced is anything but rare. In reality, the vast majority of people are weighed down with financial pressures that they struggle to overcome. Chances are you've experienced seasons like this. That may be the very reason you opened this book.

Financial challenges are so widespread that we spend about $670 million a year on financial literacy in America. There are financial books, articles, TV shows, or podcasts on just about every topic you could imagine when it comes to your money. And yet, things are only getting worse.

With so many resources already available, why would a retired banker and a pastor come together to write another book about money?

Todd Sipe spent over 40 years in the banking industry. In this role, he's had a front row seat to the challenges families face as they navigate the complexities of their personal finances. Beyond that, he understands the banking industry and knows that they can often be part of the problem. Although the banking industry claims to be there to help, they make their money when you spend your money. This is an obvious conflict of interest.

INTRODUCTION

Over 20 years ago, Todd developed a simple framework that attempted to cut through the confusion and create a clear pathway to financial health. This framework is grounded in the teachings of the Bible and is built on simple principles that are accessible and actionable. For nearly two decades, people of all ages and stages of life have implemented this framework and experienced a freedom they've never known before.

Greg Linz has served in pastoral ministry for nearly 20 years and has a deep passion to help people understand the timeless truths of Scripture. Much like Todd, he has seen the devastating effects that financial challenges can have on individuals, couples, and families. More than just causing money problems, financial stress can often lead to physical, emotional, and relational challenges. When it comes to our money, true life change isn't just about behavior modification or learning more financial information, it's about transformation of the heart.

This is what makes *Financial Purpose* different. It's more than just talking about facts and figures. By combining a practical financial framework with biblical and spiritual truths, Todd and Greg impact both the head and the heart. And that's what we need if we are going to experience true and lasting change.

In this book, you will discover what it really means to trust God. You will learn how to structure your finances in a way that actually works in our increasingly cashless world. And most importantly, you will find the joy and freedom that comes from living life as God intended.

You will notice that this book is divided into three major sections: The Foundation, The Fundamentals, and Life Applications. The Foundation and The Fundamentals sections represent the primary message. The Life

Applications section is meant as an ongoing resource that can support you through five of the most pivotal financial moments in your life.

The starting point for our journey is this: **Seek first**.

Each chapter of this book begins with scriptural foundation. And none is greater than these words from Jesus, "Seek first his kingdom and his righteousness, and all these things will be given to you as well." It's so tempting to separate our "spiritual" life from our "normal" life. But Jesus never made this distinction. Everything is spiritual.

So when it comes to our money, the starting point must be: How do we seek first His kingdom? How do we align ourselves with His way of doing things? God has given us biblical wisdom for our finances, but will we actually listen to Him? Will we truly seek first His kingdom in our finances?

We firmly believe that *Financial Purpose* could transform your life beginning today. It could transform your future. And it could even transform generations to come. But it starts with your commitment. Are you ready?

Let's go.

FINANCIAL PURPOSE

The
Foundation

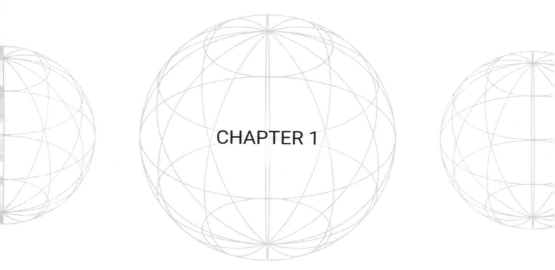

CHAPTER 1

Can I really afford the life God wants me to live?

*Trust in the Lord with all your heart
and lean not on your own understanding;
in all your ways submit to him,
and he will make your paths straight.*

Proverbs 3:5-6

Can I really afford to live the life God wants me to live?

Can I afford not to?

These are critical questions when it comes to our money. But the answer is summed up in one simple word: TRUST. Do we really trust God?

One of the most well-known passages in the Bible is found in Proverbs 3:5-6.

"Trust in the Lord with all your heart and lean not on your own understanding; in all your ways submit to him, and he will make your paths straight."

It's easy for us to read verses like this and agree with its principle. But what about when the rubber meets the road? What about the "normal" parts of our lives? What about things like our money? Have you ever looked at these words through the lens of your finances?

The first command is to, "trust in the Lord with all your heart." What does that mean? It means that the posture of your heart says, "I trust God." Not that I *will* trust God if everything works out the right way financially. Or that I *might* trust God if my financial situation changes. Or I'll *think* about trusting God if I get the right job or promotion. It is simply, "I trust God."

Trusting God means choosing to listen to His voice over every other voice. When it comes to our money, it seems like everyone has something to say. Whether it's the media, culture, or your family and friends, there are voices that are constantly trying to influence the way we relate to money. But if we truly believe in a creator God who is the source of all things, shouldn't He be the voice we care about? And since so much of the Bible talks about our money and our stuff, wouldn't it make sense to listen to what He has to say about our finances?

After challenging us to trust God, the writer of Proverbs tells us to not lean on our own understanding. It's easy to say we trust God, but if we're honest, we spend a lot of our time leaning on our own understanding. I don't know about you, but I think I'm pretty smart. I can figure stuff out on my own. But Proverbs says... *don't*. Don't try to blaze your own path. Don't try to figure it out on your own. Instead of leaning on your own understanding, submit to God. Proverbs says, "in all your ways submit to him." Even when it comes to your finances.

Some of the things we're going to talk about in this book are absolutely counter-cultural. It may even seem strange to you because it seems so different than the normal way people relate to their money. Submitting to God means trusting God enough to choose His way of doing things even if it doesn't make sense to us. Honestly, it's something we don't like to do. It means laying down our rights. It means letting God take control. But this is exactly what Proverbs commands.

Every one of us craves insight. We crave direction in our lives and would love to know God was the one guiding us. Well, we can! Proverbs 3:5-6 ends with this promise, "He will make your paths straight." If we want God's guidance, then all we need to do is trust Him enough to be guided. And when it comes to our finances, we need to be willing to let Him take control. When we do, we can be assured that the God of universe has promised to lead us. That's a pretty good deal.

No one's financial journey is perfect. We all make mistakes. We all make purchases we wish we hadn't. We all miss out on opportunities that we wish we had invested in. But the challenge is to stay in the game. Don't give up. Keep trusting. Keeping leaning on God's principles. That's what *Financial Purpose* is all about.

Exercise: Value-Based Cards

If you take time to better understand the values that drive your behavior, you can learn to make better decisions about your life and relationships.

God cares deeply about our values. We please God when we follow His Word with our thoughts and actions. Aligning your values with the life God has planned for you is the beginning of the journey.

COMPLETE THE ONLINE ACTIVITY

1.   Go to **https://www.fppathway.org/resources**

2.   Complete the **'Values Exercise'** activity on the T2P website.
3.   List your top five values:

-
-
-
-
-

CHAPTER 2

The Battle of Money

...Your will be done...

Matthew 6:10

Do you want to hear a secret?

Most people struggle with their money.

I know. It doesn't always feel like it. It feels like everyone else is doing fine and you're the only one with issues, but it's simply not true. As many as 70% of Americans are living with little or no savings [1]. That means they have no margin to deal with even the smallest strain on their finances. This leaves individuals and families who constantly find themselves growing deeper and deeper in debt. Can you relate?

Take a moment and think about the 10 closest neighbors that live around you. It doesn't matter if you live in a small apartment or a huge house. Statistics would say 7 of those 10 neighbors are currently living beyond their means. It may look like everything is great. They may be driving a nice car or they may talk to you about the new electronics they've purchased or the vacation they're about to take. But statistics would say they are in over their heads financially. If you could see their bank statements or credit card bills, you would see a completely different story than the one playing out in front of you.

What's even more eye-opening is that financial problems aren't just an issue for the young or the poor. They affect people of every age and income level. Over Todd's career as a banker, he has worked with countless people to bring financial balance to their finances. When evaluating income, most people respond that they need between 20-25% more to eliminate financial stress. What's eye-opening is how this is true no matter what someone's current income level is. The fact is no matter how much a person currently makes, most people believe the solution is to make just "a little bit more."

All of this leads us to an undeniable reality: We don't just have a money problem, we have a mindset problem.

It might surprise you that money and possessions are one of the most written about topics in the Bible. There are over 2,500 verses dedicated to addressing God's wisdom in this area. The good news is this wisdom is very clear and actionable. We can actually begin to implement it today!

The conflict is that God's wisdom flies in the face of everything our culture seems to encourage. This constant pull of culture can make God's wisdom feel foreign to us. And yet, with the toxic financial state most people find themselves in, maybe a little change would be a good thing! If you take all the wisdom found in Scripture relating to money and possessions, there are four very simple principles that become clear. This is what we will spend the bulk of our time digging into. As you'll see in the chart below, culture's message is often at odds with God's wisdom.

God's Wisdom	Culture's Message
Spend less than you make	Spend everything and more
Save with purpose	Why save when you can borrow
Beware of debt	Borrow as much as you can
Give cheerfully	Give if there is anything left over

When you look at this list, the choice seems obvious, doesn't it? Unfortunately, it doesn't matter if God's wisdom is better than culture's message. Right now, culture is winning.

78% of Americans are living paycheck to paycheck [2]

70% of Americans have little to no savings [3]

77% of Americans carry a record amount of debt [4]

Only 10-25% of church attenders give regularly [5]

The impact is painful

Health: 75% of Americans rank money as their #1 stress in life [6]

Marriage: Money is the #1 thing couples argue about [7]

Family: 73% of Americans who die today have an average debt of $62,000 [8]

Church communities: Giving in American churches is lower today than it was during the Great Depression [9]

So, what is the path forward?

Jesus gave us insight when He was teaching His disciples how to pray. In what many of us know as the Lord's Prayer, Jesus spoke these four little words, "Thy will be done." This is something Jesus expected His disciples to focus on. In a world that so often is fixated on themselves, Jesus gave us a different mindset and a different way to live. It isn't the way everyone else lives. It doesn't value the same things everyone else values. But it's the only way to experience the life God desires for us.

And "thy will be done" wasn't something Jesus just asked His disciples to do; Jesus modeled it for them. While in the garden of Gethsemane and facing imminent death, Jesus spoke those same four words to the Father. In doing so, Jesus showed His followers what this phrase really means. "Thy will be done" isn't just for the easy times, the convenient times, or the times when it guarantees a blessing. "Thy will be done" is an attitude of the heart. It's an expression of submission to the ultimate king of your life. It's a recognition that your desire is to honor God no matter the outcome.

Ordering our finances God's way is less about us receiving what we want from our money and more about God receiving what He deserves from our money. It's about putting action to the idea that Jesus is Lord of your life. For many of us, the greatest act of obedience in our lives isn't going to church or volunteering at the local non-profit. It's demonstrating submission to God with the resources He has blessed us with. It's saying no to culture's message about money and choosing to live according to God's wisdom.

Do you want to hear another secret?

Following God's wisdom is the best way to experience a healthy financial life. If we put into practice the wisdom God has given us, we will see a dramatic transformation take place in our finances. We all understand that no significant change happens overnight. It takes time. It takes intentionality. It may not always be easy. But we can be confident that God's wisdom for our finances is absolutely what is best.

Exercise: Behavior Change

Changing behavior is difficult. Successful change starts with understanding where you are prepared and where you might struggle. This exercise is for your own personal reflection on God's will, alignment with Him, and the hard work it will take.

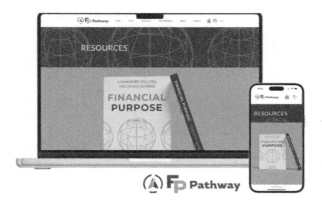

COMPLETE THE ONLINE ACTIVITY

1. Go to **https://www.fppathway.org/resources**

2. Complete the **'Readiness Assessment'** activity.
3. Download or print your report (PDF).
4. Spend time in prayer asking God for discernment.

Discussion Questions

1. Look at your top five values from the exercise from Chapter One. What clarity did this exercise bring to what you value most? How is your spending in alignment with your values? If you have a significant other, discuss how your finances currently reflect your values.

2. Review the *Readiness Assessment*. What are your greatest strengths and weaknesses as it applies to changing your money habits? If you have a significant other, compare your readiness. How can you support each other in areas of potential difficulty?

3. Compare God's wisdom and culture's view of money. Why is it so hard to follow God's wisdom with money?

4. How does following culture's view of money impact your health, marriage, family and church community? What would the impact be if you chose to follow God's wisdom instead?

Personal Reflection: The foundation of *Financial Purpose* is to seek God, trust Him and follow His will. As you reflect on Chapters One and Two, what have you discovered regarding God's word about money? What implications will this have on how you approach your finances?

The Fundamentals

CHAPTER 3

FUNDAMENTAL ONE:

Spend Less Than You Make

The wise man saves for the future,
but the foolish man spends whatever he gets.

Proverbs 21:20 TLB

Spend less than you make.

This principle is so simple and straightforward. It makes complete sense. Proverbs makes it plain for us. So why is it so ridiculously difficult to follow?

One word: Hope. We usually see hope as a good thing. Sure, hope is powerful; hope is inspiring. Our world craves and is in desperate need of hope. But when it comes to our finances, hope is a killer.

Why is that? Because *hope isn't a plan*. As Christians, we may understand God's perspective on money. We can desire to be good stewards of our resources. We can even hope to follow God's path for our finances. But if we don't make a plan, we inevitably continue down the path of overspending and end up mismanaging our finances one purchase at a time.

This is where Ann found herself. Through tears, she talked about her recent marriage and the hopes and dreams she had for their future. She wanted more kids, to own a home, and to enjoy all the adventure life could offer. But her marriage was struggling and money was the central source of their conflict. She didn't know what to do or where to turn.

As Ann continued to share, it became evident that she and her husband Drew were not on the same page. They hadn't figured out how to work together on their finances and move in the same direction. To make matters worse, her anxieties for the future and his pride made it difficult to admit they needed help. It was easy to understand why the tears were flowing. They desperately needed a new pathway forward.

Spending less than you make is Fundamental One. It takes intentionality. It takes purpose. It takes a plan. And more than just a plan, it takes a commitment to follow through with that plan. In this chapter, we unveil a financial framework that can help you think about your money and organize it in a totally new way. This framework has helped countless people experience a whole new life and it begins with three simple steps:

1. Change your financial equation
2. Separate your money
3. Track and make adjustments

CHANGE YOUR FINANCIAL EQUATION

The typical equation most people use for their finances is this:

Paycheck - debts - bills - spending = savings and giving

At first glance this seems to make sense. Think about it: The typical American receives pay each month in the form of checks, cash, or a direct deposit. That money is then generally deposited into one checking account that is used to pay debts, pay bills, and cover everyday expenses. This explains the left side of the equation. If there is any money left over at the end of the month, they can save or give. This is the right side of the equation. But let's be honest, there is rarely any money left over! And even if there is a surprise bonus or a tax refund, without a plan for that money, it's often gone before the next paycheck arrives. Society calls this "living paycheck to paycheck." God calls this being foolish.

This view of money and structure of banking creates further problems. When we co-mingle all financial activity into one bank account (in this case a checking account) it becomes difficult to keep track of what's coming in and what's going out of our account. The result is that most people ignore the details and simply check their account to see how much money is left. It's no wonder that at the end of most months, the money is gone and the cycle starts all over again. Even worse is that this financial structure doesn't give you the ability to prepare for your financial dreams and aspirations. Saving is an afterthought as expenses and spending inevitably leave you with no margin. When an irregular or unexpected expense arrives, it can mean a financial crisis because you aren't prepared.

But what if we thought about our money in a different way? What if we reorganized our financial plan and used a different equation?

Paycheck – commitments = spending

This short equation has the power to revolutionize your financial world. Obviously, it seems simpler than the previous equation, but what does it really mean? To understand this equation, we need to understand the terms.

What is a commitment? Commitments are financial obligations based on contracts, agreements, or personal goals. A financial contract is a legal obligation you are required to fulfill. Examples of this would be a loan for a home or a car payment. Agreements are just that, financial agreements to pay for goods or services. This could take on the form of utilities, a financial pledge to a non-profit, or the expenses associated with your child's music lessons or athletics. Personal goals are anything you want to prepare for or work toward financially. This might be saving for a vacation, a home remodel, or even saving up for your kid's braces.

Another way to think about commitments is by focusing on where you are making a commitment. We propose that there are three parties we make commitments to: God, ourselves, and others. Whether your commitment is an obligation, an agreement, or a goal, thinking through all three of these categories can help you clarify all of your possible commitments.

Commitments come in a variety of structures, but the most common commitment is a fixed amount paid or saved each month. Some examples would include rent/mortgage, loans, and insurance. Other monthly commitments might include things like cell phone plans, cable TV, or subscriptions to streaming services. Although some commitments are predictable fixed amounts, other commitments may vary based on usage (i.e. electricity, natural gas). In addition, some commitments may be irregular in their frequency or simply occur less frequently than monthly. Utilities like water and garbage are often paid bimonthly or even quarterly. Commitments that take the form of a personal goal (such as saving up for a new couch) can be structured however seems best to each individual.

Now that we understand what a commitment is, what is spending? Spending represents all of our day-to-day financial expenses. This includes things like food, gas, basic needs and wants. But unlike the first equation where you spend first and hope to have a little left over to save or give, this model has already taken that into account. You've already labeled things like saving and giving as commitments and have prepared for them. That means that whatever is left over can be spent without guilt or regret. This is where you really begin to feel the freedom of healthy finances. When your commitments are already funded, it makes spending more fun!

Here's an example of a new way to think about your money around commitments and spending:

Monthly Commitments		Non-Monthly Commitments		Spending	
Auto Pmt	$352.85	Garbage	$11.67	Food	$500.00
Utilities	$225.11	Water	$66.67	Restaurant	$300.00
Cell/Internet	$122.76	Car Insurance	$100.00	Gas	$300.00
Mortgage	$2,480.06	Property Tax	$300.00	Entertainment	$250.00
Church Tithe (10%)	$1,000.00				
Missions	$50.00				
Monthly Totals	$4,230.78		$478.34		$1,350.00

Now that you understand the difference between commitments and spending, we turn to step two.

SEPARATE YOUR MONEY

Clarifying commitments and spending is great, but now what? We put that knowledge into action.

As was shared earlier, most people have just one checking account and sometimes a savings account. However, to take full advantage of this framework, we recommend setting up three checking accounts and one savings account (see illustration below). In order to make transferring between accounts most seamless, we recommend setting up all accounts with the same bank.

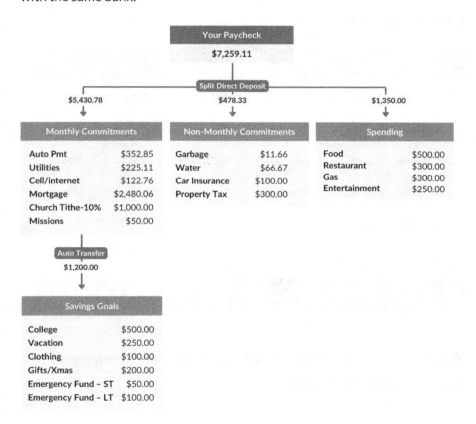

You're probably thinking, "why in the world do I need four bank accounts?" We get it. It may seem excessive. And it will require some effort to get all the accounts set up to use this framework. But once this has been completed and you have leveraged the power of automation within your accounts, you will have freedom in your finances like never before. Not only will you have confidence knowing your commitments are funded, but ensuring your commitments are taken care of first will allow you to engage in guilt-free spending.

What are all those accounts used for? Let's dig in.

The first checking account is for your **monthly commitments**. As described above, these are any commitments that have a monthly expectation. If you take the time, you can calculate to the penny what your fixed monthly obligations are. In addition to your loans and bills, this should include any giving commitments you've made. Make sure to account for any variance in monthly utilities by taking the average amount for the year.

Once you have determined the cost of each of your monthly commitments, add them all together to determine your total monthly commitments. Then, divide that number by the amount of paychecks you receive each month (generally one or two per month). This is the amount that needs to be deposited into your first checking account each paycheck. If you are paid every two weeks (26 paychecks per year), our recommendation is to live off of 24 paychecks (two per month) and use the extra two paychecks each year for debt reduction and savings.

To fund each of your accounts, our recommendation is to utilize direct deposit. Many employers are willing to divide the payment of your paycheck into different accounts. Doing this will make things even easier for you to ensure that your accounts are being funded regularly. If your employer is unwilling to make multiple direct deposits on your behalf, you can set up one direct deposit of your whole check and then have your bank make automatic transfers from that account to the others to ensure each account is funded.

The timing of your expenses within the month is something that needs to be addressed. Some bills come due at the beginning of the month, while others may come due later in the month. If you are not prepared for this, you may not have your account funded in time. There are two ways to address this. Some companies are willing to change the due date for your payments by simply making a call and asking. If this isn't a good solution, then you may need to deposit additional money initially to ensure you have enough funds to cover the first month's expenses.

Since these expenses are fixed and monthly, set up bill pay or automatic payment for all these commitments. Once set up, this account will run on autopilot. Both deposits and payments are made automatically and you will never have to sit down and pay these monthly bills again. Sounds nice, doesn't it?

The second checking account is for **non-monthly commitments**. These are budget-busters and can kill your monthly cash flow. They include all predictable payments that are not monthly. This can include semi-monthly, quarterly, semi-annual or annual payments such as quarterly garbage bills, semi-annual homeowner or auto insurance, annual car registration, or yearly membership payments. In addition, this may include irregular but predictable expenses such as lawn care, children's sports, or pet grooming and vet expenses. Any commitment that you know you will need to pay can be accounted for in this category.

Once you've determined what your non-monthly commitments are, you will need to figure out the total cost of funding them. Take the total yearly cost of each commitment and add them all together. This will give you the total yearly cost of all your non-monthly commitments. Then, divide that number by the amount of paychecks you receive in a calendar year (12 or

24). This will be the amount you will need to deposit in your second checking account every pay period to ensure that you have enough money to cover your expenses.

As a reminder, if you receive 26 paychecks each year, we recommend living off of 24 paychecks (2 per month) and using the extra two paychecks for debt reduction and savings. Using the same concept of direct deposit, have your employer deposit this amount of your paycheck in this checking account. Again, timing may be an issue. It may be necessary to deposit additional funds into this account initially to ensure there is enough money when the expenses are accrued.

Typically, payments and expenses in this category can also be paid using bill pay or automatic payment. If you have taken the time to fully prepare for all non-monthly commitments and set up automatic payments, you will never be surprised by a forgotten bill again! Also, by setting up your accounts with direct deposit, auto-transfers, and bill pay, it's possible you may not need checks or a debit card for one or both of your first two checking accounts.

The third checking account is for **spending**. This is the money you have left over after accounting for your commitments. This includes items such as food, clothing, entertainment, gas, and other miscellaneous items. In our increasingly cashless world, you typically use your debit card to spend money from this account.

This is the most important account to pay attention to. Day to day expenses aren't fixed, so it's necessary to monitor how much money is in the account and adjust your decisions accordingly. *The key is to avoid spending more than you have before your next paycheck.* If you have a fixed salary, then the amount deposited is predictable. If your pay is variable due to working hourly or on commission, you will need to take a bit more time planning how to account for this. Either way, you must be careful to only spend what you have in your account. If you know you will need more money for a weekend event, you may need to keep expenses down during the week. If you have an expensive week full of activities, you may need to reduce the coming weekend's activities to compensate. Within a few weeks of monitoring and adjusting, you'll get the hang of it. Just stay with it!

The **savings account** is for exactly that: Savings. The next chapter will dig deeper into this area, but the primary purpose of savings is to prepare for more significant needs. Maybe you need to prepare for emergencies or lost income due to job loss, medical leave, or reduced hours. Maybe you've set goals for items like vacation, a down payment for a car/home, or even your child's college education. The key is to assign a purpose to every dollar you save.

Like everything else in this framework, saving requires intentionality. Savings goals are commitments you make to yourself. In order to fund these goals, follow the same process as non-monthly commitments. Add up the yearly total for all of your savings goals to determine your total savings necessary. Then, divide the total number by the amount of paychecks you receive in a calendar year (usually 12 or 24). As with the other accounts, utilizing direct deposit or bank transfers to automate your saving will make things more consistent and intentional.

That is it.

You might be asking yourself, how is this framework any different from a budget? We're glad you asked!

Budgets are based on an estimate of how much money you *think* you will have and need to spend. If reality doesn't line up with your budget, then you have to start all over again. This framework is based on the *actual* expenses and money you do have. It is grounded on the understanding that you can only spend the money you currently have, period.

TRACK AND MAKE ADJUSTMENTS

Now that you understand the difference between commitments and spending, and have separated your money into different accounts, you are ready for the final step: Track and make adjustments.

This step involves reviewing your monthly and non-monthly accounts periodically to ensure that your expenses are staying on track and that each of your accounts are funded enough to cover your commitments. In addition, you must consistently monitor your spending account as this is your allowance for your everyday expenses. The most exciting part of utilizing this framework is watching your savings steadily grow and gain momentum. Through patience and endurance you can begin to see your goals become reality.

Life is dynamic; it is always changing. There is no way to predict the future. The same is true of our finances, for good or bad. You may experience a job change, receive a raise, have another child, suffer a medical emergency, need to replace an appliance, or any one of an infinite number of possibilities. Life happens. And with every change, it's important to adjust.

Remember, this framework is intended to help you with the money you have, not the money you wish you had. With every change that takes place in your finances, you will need to make an adjustment in some way. If a change results in a pay increase, then make an intentional decision about what you are going to do with that additional money and adjust your framework accordingly. This may mean that you can increase how much you save or increase your spending. However, if the change results in an increase in one of your commitments, then you will have to make a trade off somewhere in your framework to account for this. Similarly, if you find yourself struggling to get by with the amount of money remaining in your spending account each paycheck, you will need to adjust your commitments to create more margin for day-to-day expenses.

The difference between someone who starts things and someone who finishes things is perseverance. Leveraging this framework in your personal finances can change your life, but it will take work. And sometimes it will require sacrifices and hard decisions. But if the goal is to pursue God's best in our finances, isn't it worth it?

Two years after working with Ann and Drew to set up a financial plan, they requested that we meet again. Oftentimes, people struggle to follow through with their plan and will come back to start over. Committing to this framework through the pressures of life and culture is challenging. It is so easy to get off track. Honestly, it is very common to need multiple starting points in your financial story. The key is to never give up and keep pressing on.

When Ann and Drew walked into the room, they had a different presence. The conversation wasn't about their financial difficulties and relational pain. Instead, Drew reached out his hand to shake mine, and with a warm look in his eye said, "Thank you. Thanks for changing my life, our marriage, and our family. Without the framework you introduced to us, we would not have survived as a married couple. Today, we are expecting another child and we are applying for our first-time home loan, three years ahead of plan."

What will your story look like?

Exercise: Spending Framework

Do you know where you are spending your money today? Don't worry, most people do not. This exercise is designed to help you find out. It may be the hardest part, but it's worth the effort!

COMPLETE THE ONLINE ACTIVITY

1. Go to **https://www.fppathway.org/resources**

2. Launch the **'FP Calculator'** and complete the **Chapter 3 'Spend'** section.

3. As you create your lists, identify your current spending amounts to the best of your ability, using exact amounts where you can. If you are unsure, don't worry. Just start with a reasonable amount. You will fine-tune the numbers by the end of Section 2.

Discussion Questions

1. What did you learn about the differences between commitments and spending?

2. How do you feel about separating your money into four bank accounts? What questions do you have?

3. How have you monitored your money up until this point? How does the new framework change the way you monitor?

Personal Reflection: The wise man saves, but the foolish man spends whatever he gets. As you reflect on Chapter Three, what have you discovered regarding God's Word about money? What implication will this have on how you approach your spending?

CHAPTER 4

FUNDAMENTAL TWO:

Save With Purpose

*The wise man saves for the future,
but the foolish man spends whatever he gets.*

Proverbs 21:20 TLB

You may be thinking to yourself, didn't we just look at that verse?

Well, yes. We did. But it's just too simple and important not to repeat: "The wise man saves for the future, but the foolish man spends whatever he gets."

But if it's that simple, why is saving money still so hard? The short answer is: We spend too much. If we have too much debt, it's usually because we spend too much. If we struggle to be generous, it's usually because we spend too much. And if we aren't saving any money, it's usually because we spend too much. Until we get a handle on Fundamental One, it's impossible to achieve the remaining fundamentals. But when we master Fundamental One, a whole new world of financial possibilities becomes available to us and we can be better prepared for whatever life throws our way. Todd's and Barb's daughter, Maggie, proved how true this really is.

Maggie is the youngest of four children in her family. As with every "baby" of the family, there were benefits and challenges. When you get to the fourth child, parents have often learned from their mistakes and the youngest child reaps the benefits. However, when parents get to their last child, they are older and frankly, may be less energetic. This was true for Maggie. In fact, she had an earlier curfew than her older siblings did simply because Todd and Barb, couldn't stay up as late as they used to!

When it came to teaching their children about money, Todd and Barb started early and reinforced the four fundamentals all the way through their early life events. They also helped each child set up their own framework to manage their money by the time they were 16. Each of their children had mastered this by the time they left for college. That is, everyone except for Maggie. Although she had her framework, she didn't really use it or fully understand it. And although Todd and Barb had taken the time to try and help Maggie with her framework in both high school and college, they didn't really put the energy in like they had with their other children.

When Maggie graduated college and secured her first job, her finances were in good shape. She didn't have any debt and she had plenty of savings. However, a few conversations with Maggie left Todd concerned that she wasn't going to put in the time or focus necessary on the fundamentals to continue down a path of financial health. Your twenties are a critical season of life and without the fundamentals in place, Todd feared that Maggie's road would be more difficult than it needed to be.

All of this changed during the Covid-19 pandemic of 2020. The tumultuous season the world went through left everyone struggling to figure out how to best manage their finances through a challenging circumstance. No one was fully prepared for how to deal with the uncertainty. But it was this pressure that brought the best out of Maggie.

Maggie lived with a couple of roommates and they noticed something different in the way she was handling a trying season. Despite suffering a major drop in income, she continued to survive financially when others were struggling to keep their head above water. When they approached her about this, Maggie the student became Maggie the teacher.

Maggie shared the concepts of commitments and spending that we learned in Chapter Three and explained the framework for organizing her money. She took the time to help each of her roommates set up their own framework so they could be equipped for their own financial health. And most importantly, Maggie talked about the fact that because she had saved money in the event she ever had a loss of income, she was able to continue living fairly normally until her income rebounded. Suffice it to say, this was a proud parenting moment for Todd and Barb. But even more so, it was a life-changing moment for Maggie's roommates.

Saving money is the second fundamental for a very specific reason. It's an absolute must. Without savings, any unanticipated financial pressure can result in a major financial crisis. This means that even if you've set up your framework, without any savings set aside, you could find yourself unprepared for the unexpected. But with a little intentionality and preparation, your savings can help you weather the financial storms that will inevitably come. Also, savings is what allows you to achieve the goals and dreams you have for your life and future.

But having savings in your bank account isn't enough by itself. The real goal is to apply purpose to that savings so that you can manage your personal priorities as well as the challenges that come your way. Purpose with your savings will grow by following these three principles:

1. Assign a purpose to every dollar saved

2. Automate your saving

3. Live within your framework and save everything else

ASSIGN A PURPOSE TO EVERY DOLLAR SAVED

Saving money may seem like an easy task. The problem is that once you have money saved, how do you make sure it just doesn't turn back into spending money? We all deal with a similar weakness we like to call our "marginal propensity to spend." The more money we have, the more often our wants become needs. And the more money we have in our savings account, the more we want to use it to buy the things we really desire. You may *want* a new TV, but when you have money in your savings account you feel the *need* to have a new TV. The more margin we have, the more we want to spend.

The key to avoiding this trap is to assign a purpose to every dollar saved. Instead of just having a lump sum of money sitting in a savings account, you now have separated your savings into categories that represent your priorities or goals. For example, your account might look like this:

Savings account balance: $12,000

Purposes:

Kids college: $1,500

Vacation: $1,000

Emergency fund: $4,500

Down-payment for home: $5,000

By separating your money, you are able to see that every dollar spent from savings has a trade-off. Imagine you are walking through the electronics department and you see the TV you want. If all you think about is the $12,000 sitting in savings, it's easy to justify the expense. But by assigning a purpose to every dollar, you are now left with a decision. If you want to buy the TV, you will have to take the money from one of your savings categories. Once you have decided the category to take the money from, the question becomes, "is the TV worth the trade-off?" By taking the step of assigning a purpose to every dollar saved, you can now make a more informed decision about your purchases.

It's important to remember that the money in your savings account is your money. You can do what you want with it. You can buy that TV, the new car, or whatever you like. But the key is to realize that every financial decision has consequences. Every dollar spent in one area cannot be used in another area. Every decision has a trade-off. Is it worth it? You get to decide.

When planning your savings, it's also important to realize you should plan for both short-term and long-term goals. Short-term goals might be things like an emergency fund, vacation, or new furniture. Long-term goals are often bigger and require more forethought. When it comes to long-term savings, the "Big 3" are retirement, health care, and children's college. Below are a few tips for these areas of savings:

RETIREMENT

Put 10-15% of your paycheck directly into a retirement account. If you do this for the entirety of your working career, you will be set up to retire.

HEALTH CARE

If you have access to a Health Savings Account, fund it with the maximum amount. This becomes tax free money for you.

COLLEGE

Open a 529 savings plan when your child is born. By making a monthly contribution to that account, you will be able to prepare for one of the biggest expenses your child will ever face.

AUTOMATE YOUR SAVING

By this point, it's clear that if you don't make a plan to save, you will inevitably end up spending that money. Saving your money doesn't happen by accident, it takes intentionality.

The framework we learned about in Chapter Three gave us the lens to view our savings as a commitment to ourselves. If we are waiting until there is a little extra to save, we will be waiting forever. The key is to systematically build our savings plan into our framework. By automating your saving every time you are paid, you will begin to see a steady growth toward your goals and priorities.

In addition to the basic automation of regularly allocating income to savings, it's helpful to take advantage of other means to increase saving. Many banks offer programs that will automatically transfer small amounts into a savings account by rounding up your credit card or debit card transactions to the nearest dollar and transferring that amount into savings. Also, utilizing payroll benefits such as a 401k or Health Savings Accounts are other great ways to leverage automation to increase your savings.

The key to saving is to do it intentionally. By automating your saving, you will fund your priorities and reach your goals more quickly. This means your dreams don't have to stay dreams.

LIVE WITHIN YOUR FRAMEWORK AND SAVE EVERYTHING ELSE

There's a term we use that doesn't sound exciting: Self-control. It seems so boring. But this is exactly what you need to achieve the goals you have in your life. Once you've established your framework to prepare for your normal commitments and spending, your self control will be tested. What do you do when you receive that extra income, unplanned bonus, tax refund, or gift?

Whenever unexpected money comes in, it's an opportunity to fuel the priorities you've already established. If you've set savings goals, unexpected income becomes an opportunity to reach those goals more quickly. Deposit that money into savings and assign a purpose to it. If you don't, your marginal propensity to spend will cause that extra cash to vanish.

Todd and Barb learned this lesson a little late with their children. When their oldest child Chris started high school, they attended the freshman orientation. During the session, one topic presented was preparing your child for college. With four kids, who had time to ever think about future things like saving for college? But their lack of preparation hit them like a two-by-four across the forehead in that meeting. They realized they only had four years to try and prepare for their son's college.

What did they do? They made a commitment to save all extra money and place it into a 529 plan for their kids. This was a difficult decision and required consistent sacrifices. All extra money was invested in their kids' future. Putting four kids through college meant 16 years of college expenses over a 14-year-period of time. That was a heavy burden. By exercising self-control and saving everything they could, they were able to accomplish their goal of helping all of their children with college.

Self-control may not be a defining characteristic of your finances. Living like this may even seem strange to you. And if you look at the way most people treat their money, it is strange. But as we've learned, the normal way of relating to money leaves people in debt, stressed out, and overwhelmed.

Maybe a little self-control is just what you need!

Exercise: Saving With Purpose

Assigning a purpose to every dollar in savings is important. But where do you start? How do you keep track? Between the FP Calculator and FP Goal Tracker, we've got you covered!

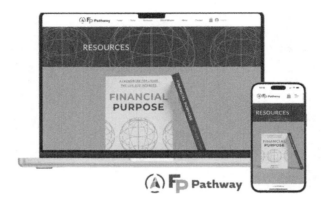

COMPLETE THE ONLINE ACTIVITY

1. Go to **https://www.fppathway.org/resources**

2. Launch the **'FP Calculator'** and complete the **Chapter 4 'Save'** section.
3. Go back to the **'Resources'** page and launch the **'FP Goal Tracker'** and explore how you can keep track of savings goals.

Discussion Questions

1. What are the implications of assigning a purpose to every dollar of savings?

2. How do you systematically save today? Are there any new apps or other technology you are using to save money?

3. List all the potential ways additional money comes in throughout the year. Include side hustles, tax refunds, bonus, rebates, etc. Since your framework is set with your commitments and spending, what are your thoughts on the best use of these additional funds?

Personal Reflection: The wise man saves but the foolish man spends whatever he gets. As you reflect on Chapter Four, what have you discovered regarding God's word about money? What implication will this have on how you approach your savings?

CHAPTER 5

FUNDAMENTAL THREE:

Beware of Debt

The rich rule over the poor,
and the borrower is slave to the lender.

Proverbs 22:7

Many people in our world view the Christian life as restrictive.

Like a straightjacket that holds you down, they view God's laws and guidance as something that sucks the fun out of life. In reality, God's laws and guidance are more like a life vest. They're protective. God's desire is to keep us away from the things that will ultimately enchain and destroy us.

Enter Fundamental Three: Beware of Debt.

There may be nothing more suffocating and nothing that causes more mental anguish than financial debt. Debt can truly enslave you and keep you from living the life of financial freedom God desires for you. And yet, nearly everyone struggles with debt.

As we have seen throughout this book, not everyone who says they have your interests in mind are doing what's best for you. There is no place where this is more clear than when it comes to debt. Banks make their money when you spend money. They make even more money when you borrow their money. For this reason, it's in the interest of the bank or lending agency to help you borrow as much money as you are allowed to, even if it isn't wise.

Because of this, it's important to not only beware of how much money you borrow, but also who you borrow money from. If the bank you work with is most interested in making money off of your transaction rather than helping you do what's best, then that may lead you to ask a very dangerous question: How much money *can* I borrow? If your lending agency actually cares about you, they will help you ask a much better question: How much money *should* I borrow? Asking the wrong question can lead you down the same road Troy and Candace found themselves on.

Troy and Candace walked into Todd's office buried in financial debt and struggling to get out. For their first meeting, Candace wouldn't even show up because she was so embarrassed and filled with shame about their circumstance. However, Todd's rule is that he only works with couples if both parties are present and engaged. Financial challenges can only be dealt with when a couple is working together.

After rescheduling the meeting, they all met together at a local coffee shop. When Todd walked in, he found Troy and Candace already seated and clearly very tense. As the conversation began, Candace was tentative and withdrawn from the conversation. Todd's first question to couples is often the same, "What do you hope to get out of our time together?" Candace couldn't even answer the question because she couldn't begin to imagine a way out of their predicament.

As is often the case, the more they talked, the more Candace's story began to unfold. Debt wasn't a new challenge for Candace. It was a long-term issue that had negatively impacted her first marriage and was now leading her to the brink of another divorce. Troy and Candace's debt problem was consuming Candace's mind and emotions. All she wanted to do was bury her head and pretend it didn't exist. What was so sad was that between the two of them, Troy and Candace had a significant income.

Debt can affect anyone. And it can be devastating. In order to navigate the risk of debt, there are three important principles:

1. Identify and eliminate your bad debt
2. Manage your debt-to-income ratio
3. Set a goal to be debt-free

IDENTIFY AND ELIMINATE YOUR BAD DEBT

Not all debt is bad. There is such a thing as good debt. However, our culture is filled with opportunities to take on bad debt and it's extremely important to understand the difference.

Good debt is debt that helps generate income and build your net worth. This can include things like homeownership, dependable transportation, and investing in your education or career. Conversely, bad debt stems from purchases that don't increase in value or generate income. This includes things like credit card debt, home equity loans, and financing for most consumable purchases. Using debt for things that are consumed or depreciate in value is not wise.

The cause of debt isn't the only thing that makes debt good or bad. The structure of debt can make a huge difference in whether the debt is good or bad. A poorly structured loan can turn good debt into bad debt and have painful results for your long-term financial health. Let's look at a few examples.

HOMEOWNERSHIP

Homeownership can be great, but it isn't for everyone. Investing in a home takes discipline. Not only is it necessary to manage your loan payments, but it's also necessary to maintain your home and save money to fund the ongoing maintenance that a property requires. For the vast majority of people, homeownership is a wise investment.

Owning a home can bring joyful memories to your family and become one of the most valuable assets in your financial plan.

When taking a long view, homes typically go up in value. Although a home mortgage is structured over many years, there is an end date. Through faithful diligence, you can own your home with no debt in retirement. This is a wise dream for every homeowner.

As we have already shared, the structure of your mortgage can turn a wise investment into a painful situation. Here are a few tips for healthy homeownership:

- Pick the shortest term you can afford. Most people pick a 30-year mortgage regardless of their situation. 30 years might be reasonable for a first-time home buyer. But as you get older and upgrade your home, it is wise to be more aggressive with paying off your debt. Consider a 15-year mortgage or even less.

- The only reason to refinance is to lower your interest rate. Do not refinance to lower your payment or add more debt to your loan. The goal in refinancing is to shorten the time remaining on your mortgage or to lower the overall cost of your loan.

- Avoid home equity loans as they eat away at the equity you have built up.

- Make sure to set money aside for home repairs and maintenance. Doing this will protect the value of your home without incurring additional debt.

DEPENDABLE TRANSPORTATION

For many, modern life requires dependable transportation. This is what enables us to commute to and from all events in life, from our jobs to our leisure activities. The danger comes when we make purchases that are less about function and more about our status. This can lead us to purchasing vehicles that we can't really afford and result in life-altering debt.

Buying a car with saved funds is clearly the best option. This frees you from additional monthly payments and allows you to increase your ability to save and give. But if you need more dependable transportation and do not have enough money saved to make a purchase, a car loan can make sense.

Much like the structure of a mortgage, the terms of a car loan are critical. Here are a few tips:

- Shop around for the lowest rates and fees for your loan. The convenience of financing through the dealer is tempting, but you may end up paying more.
- Know the total amount before committing to a purchase. Things like extra features, vehicle warranty, and taxes can add thousands of dollars to the purchase price.
- Pick the shortest repayment term you can afford. We recommend three years for a used car and five years for a new car as the maximum length of a loan. If you can't afford that, choose a less expensive vehicle.
- Remember to set aside money for car repairs and required maintenance. This will protect the value of your car and keep it

in good working condition without incurring additional debt when there is an emergency.

EDUCATION

Investing in education can be wise for accomplishing your life goals as it pertains to your career, income, or general sense of accomplishment. When taking the step to borrow money, the key is to balance your educational and professional dreams with the financial reality following the completion of your program. It's important to look beyond graduation and project the realistic income you'll earn to repay your incurred educational debt.

There are countless examples of people graduating with $100,000+ of school debt with the goal of achieving a job with a starting wage of $40,000 or less. There is no efficient way for someone to deal with that much debt on that little income. The result is being forced to refinance a student loan into a long-term repayment plan (up to 25 years). This means being enslaved to school debt for a very long time.

CREDIT CARD DEBT

Credit card debt is bad debt. The rates and fees, along with the small payment requirements, turn small purchases on a credit card into expensive transactions. In addition to this, study after study conducted on credit card purchases prove that buying things with a credit card will result in spending 18-20% more per transaction than paying cash. [10]

Many companies promote the use of credit cards to earn rewards points. While this can be a benefit for some, it can be a trap for others. If you have the money to pay your bill off completely each month, then using a credit card to earn points can be advantageous. However, if you do not pay off your purchases fully each month, you will end up paying fees and interest that far exceed any rewards you may receive.

ONE FINAL THOUGHT

Investing in things that build value and equity or investing in things that will help you produce more income are reasonable uses of debt. However, you must be careful who you borrow money from. Pick a lender whose advice matches your goals and wishes. If any lender pushes you to stretch the amount you are borrowing or the length of the repayment, then they probably don't have your best interests in mind. That loan may be good for them, but it will hurt you in the long run.

MANAGE YOUR DEBT-TO-INCOME RATIO

First things first: What is a debt-to-income ratio? This ratio compares the amount of debt you owe with the amount of income you earn. While understanding this ratio is helpful for managing your finances, it is critical to understand it because the banking industry uses it when considering possible financing options.

Determining your debt-to-income (D/I) ratio is a relatively simple and straightforward calculation. Add up all of your monthly loan payments including rent or mortgage. Divide that number by your total gross monthly income.

Total monthly loan payments / Gross monthly income = D/I ratio

Since this ratio is one bankers use regularly, let's dig in a little deeper to understand how it impacts you.

Fundamentally, banks are a source of money. They help you keep your money safe and offer options to finance items you can't pay cash for. But you need to understand something clearly: Banks don't care how much money you save or give. It sounds brutal, but it's true.

This is where the debt-to-income ratio comes in. The banking industry knows how much money they can lend you and safely expect to receive the money back. Let's call that the maximum threshold. Their goal is to enable you to borrow as much as possible up until you reach that maximum threshold. Why do they want to lend you so much money? Because this is how *they* make money. The interest and fees you pay when you borrow money yields high returns for banks. Your debt is funding their profit.

Like all businesses, banks have shareholders and investors who expect to receive a profit. Despite what banks want you to believe, your financial health is *not* their primary goal. Their primary goal is to make a profit. Clearly, this is a conflict of interest. Understanding this conflict is critical to making wise financial decisions. Your long-term financial health requires you to surround yourself with people who will look out for your best interests.

The banking industry has established 43% as the maximum threshold for your debt-to-income ratio. This would mean that 43% of your gross income would go toward paying your debt. As we will see in a moment, this is a dangerous level of debt. Despite the excessiveness of this ratio, banks are really good at approving you for the maximum amount of debt possible. Combine this with a culture who is constantly encouraging us to buy the biggest house, the newest car, or the latest electronic and it's no surprise that we are burdened with a toxic amount of debt.

Not everyone loves math in school. But looking at a little math will help you understand why the maximum threshold of debt is foolish and unsustainable. For the average person, if you combine a 43% debt-to-income ratio with standard federal and state income taxes, as much as 70% of your income is gone before you even start living. Nationally, we spend 33% of our income on living expenses (food, clothing, entertainment, etc.).

Debt-to-income ratio:	43%
Taxes:	27%
Spending:	33%
Total:	103%

You don't have to be a mathematician to understand this doesn't work. Living with a debt-to-income ratio of 43% is irrational. Not only does it leave you in a deficit each month which produces even more debt, it leaves you no margin to deal with the inevitable emergencies that come up in life. On top of that, this level of debt leaves you no ability to save or give. And despite all this, the banking industry will often enable people to take on this level of debt.

Throughout Todd's 40+ years in banking, the debt-to-income ratio has crept higher and higher. Forty years ago, bankers were valued and respected in their communities. Bankers encouraged people to save their money and discouraged excessive borrowing. Most banks were owned by someone who resided in the community and cared about the success of their community. They understood that the financial health of a community is based on the financial health of its families.

Unfortunately, this mindset in the banking industry has come and gone. Through mergers and acquisitions, most banks today are owned by a large corporation. Under this new paradigm, it's no longer about building healthy families and communities. The key metric for measuring success in most banks is creating a high return for their shareholders. Their success is no longer tied to your personal success.

So, what's the correct debt-to-income ratio? Obviously, lower is better, especially when it comes to bad debt. But using the numbers we crunched above, anything above 30% makes it difficult to ever bring balance to your financial life. Studies[11] have shown that one of the greatest differentiators between those who are able to build wealth and those who struggle to live paycheck to paycheck is the amount of debt you have. Choosing to live within this guideline will take self-control, but it will enable you to avoid the financial bondage of excessive debt.

SET A GOAL TO BE DEBT-FREE

If debt is dangerous, then it only makes sense to pay off all debt as quickly as possible. But how? There are three critical steps.

First, stop acquiring new debt. That sounds obvious, but it doesn't happen by accident. Remember, you didn't set out to get into debt.

Therefore, getting out of debt is going to take work and intentionality. To control your spending, you need to learn to say no to all unnecessary purchases. If it isn't a need, then it's a no. Accomplishing this often means getting rid of credit cards. Whether you cut them up and close the accounts, or simply take them out of your wallet and store them, do whatever you need to in order to prevent new debt from being added.

Second, use your framework to manage your money and create margin that can be applied toward debt. In most cases, you will need to make sacrifices if you want to eliminate debt. You may need to cancel a subscription, return a recent purchase, postpone that vacation or delay the new car you desire. Making a sacrifice in the present can make a huge impact on your future. And when you do receive that extra bonus or unexpected income, applying it to debt reduction can help accelerate the process of getting out of debt.

Finally, as you find more money to apply against your loans, use a debt reduction method called "snowball" to accelerate paying off your loans. If you have more than one account, pay off the accounts starting with the smallest balance first, while paying the minimum payment on larger debts. Once the smallest debt is paid off, extra money from the paid account is applied to the next larger account, and continue until the largest account is paid. For directions, see: en.wikipedia.org/wiki/Debt_snowball_method

Troy and Candace didn't see a way out. And the mountain of debt they were staring at left them feeling overwhelmed and hopeless. But they leveraged the wisdom of the framework to separate their money into monthly commitments, non-monthly commitments, and spending. While walking through the exercise on needs and wants, they made some tough decisions and altered their lifestyle so that they could free up cash and pay off their debt more quickly. The burden of their debt began to lift when they started to see a pathway out.

One of the most rewarding moments in financial counseling is watching a couple gain a shared financial goal and begin working together. Once Troy and Candace had gained clarity with their framework, it enabled them to pursue alignment in their thinking. They began to dream together and establish clear goals for their future together. Instead of contemplating divorce in the coming months, they set the goal of being debt-free within three years and becoming homeowners within five years.

The morning after their first meeting with Todd, Candace called in. With a tearful voice she said, "Thank you. Last night was the first time I've had a good night's sleep in years."

Exercise: Debt Awareness

Debt can be overwhelming. Identifying all your debt is an important first step. This exercise is designed to start a plan to eliminate bad debt with the goal of becoming debt-free. Unrealistic? It is unless you start.

COMPLETE THE ONLINE ACTIVITY

1. Go to **https://www.fppathway.org/resources**

2. Launch the **'FP Calculator'** and complete the **Chapter 5 'Debt'** section.
3. List your D/I ratio _____%

Discussion Questions

1.   What surprises you the most about your list of debts?

2.   How much bad debt did you identify? If you eliminated all of your bad debt payments, what would be your D/I ratio?

3.   Are any of the loans listed as good debt potentially bad debt in disguise due to poor loan structure? If so, explain how the structure turns them into bad debt. Is there a way to change them into good debt?

4.   List the ways you can accelerate paying off your loans in order to lower your payments to under a 30% D/I ratio.

Personal Reflection: Beware of Debt. As you reflect on Chapter Five, what have you discovered regarding God's word about borrowing money? What implication will this have on how you approach your debt?

CHAPTER 6

FUNDAMENTAL FOUR:

Above All,
Give Cheerfully

*Each of you should give what you have
decided in your heart to give,
not reluctantly or under compulsion,
for God loves a cheerful giver.*

2 Corinthians 9:7

There's one word in every two-year-old's vocabulary: Mine.

Without fail, every child is consumed with themselves. We're all programmed that way. And this hardwiring doesn't naturally change as we get older. Whether it's more toys as a kid or more cash in our 401k as adult, it's so easy to only care about ourselves. But God's plan for your life is so much grander than that.

Above all, give cheerfully. This final fundamental is the easiest to understand and the easiest to accomplish. The simple question is: Will we actually do it?

Scripture makes it abundantly clear that God loves a cheerful giver. But it's easy to think, "That's just because God wants all of my money." But you have to remember, He's God. He owns everything, He doesn't need your money! It's also possible to think, "God wants me to give because of the impact my finances can make." While it's true there are countless worthy organizations that could benefit from your financial investment, that also isn't the reason God challenges us to give.

The real reason God loves a cheerful giver is because of what giving does to our hearts. Jesus said this in Matthew 6:21, "For where your treasure is, there your heart will be also." How we manage our money will affect our heart, for good or bad. When we operate with selfishness and stinginess, it puts us in chains and makes our world small. When we operate with generosity, it literally sets us free and transforms us to look more and more like our Father in Heaven.

Generosity also impacts our outlook on the world and challenges us in the way we love and care for the people and communities around us. When we start to embody God's generosity in our own life, we begin to realize there is a joy in giving that is unbelievably contagious. In time, generosity often becomes the most impactful and fulfilling part of our financial life. To encourage cheerful giving, follow these three principles:

1. Make giving your first commitment
2. Begin where you are
3. Let God work within your heart

MAKE GIVING YOUR FIRST COMMITMENT

In Chapter Three, we learned all about commitments and spending. When you make giving your first commitment, it turns giving from an afterthought to a priority. In a practical sense, this ensures that the value of giving is built into your finances on the front end. In time, you will learn what it looks like to live on what is remaining.

However, giving to God as your first commitment has a much deeper effect. When we choose to give of our first and our best to God, we learn what it really means to trust Him. It becomes a constant reminder that our source is not our job, retirement account or wallet. Our source is God alone. For many of us, the greatest step of faith we can take is to regularly put God first in our finances.

BEGIN WHERE YOU ARE

Many people think that the reason they aren't very generous is because they simply don't have enough money. They may think to themselves, "If I had more, I would give more." But is that actually the case? In the parable of the talents, Jesus reveals that our current level of faithfulness is an indicator of our future behavior. When it comes to generosity, begin where you are.

Choosing to give requires us to go back to our framework and make some decisions. The first decision is how much can or should you give. That's a decision between you and God. If you've never engaged in consistent giving, then start giving something. Once you've decided how much to give, it's time to go back to your framework. Make the necessary adjustments to ensure you are able to fulfill all of your commitments with enough money left for spending.

LET GOD WORK WITHIN YOUR HEART

Generosity isn't just a moment in time; it's a journey. When we consistently choose generosity, God shapes our hearts more and more to look like His. *The result is that giving transforms from a thing we do into who we are.*

Todd and Barb set up a framework shortly after they got married. In fact, the decision to organize their finances was birthed out of their first big fight. Barb wanted new work attire and Todd wanted new golf shoes. Guess who won? The correct answer is: No one. Fighting about money issues is painful within marriage and only leads to deeper problems.

When they initially set up their framework, giving was imbedded into their "monthly commitment account." They gave to their church, the United Way, and a few other organizations that they were connected to. As requests came in throughout the year, they typically had enough money to lean in and help. During those first few years, they were reactionary at best. They weren't really prepared for opportunities that fell outside of their monthly commitments.

As God continued to bless them financially and work within their hearts, Todd and Barb made a fundamental change in the way they looked at giving. They decided to move their giving money into a separate account. Yes, this meant creating a fourth checking account. But this little change made a huge difference as they desired to grow in their generosity.

Todd and Barb challenged themselves to double the amount they gave and to fund their account each month. They wanted to continue with their regular giving commitments but felt the desire to help more people. As the first year progressed, the money in their giving account kept growing and growing. Although they changed how much they were going to give, they were still dependent on organizations asking for money.

As the year ended, they decided to make a change from being reactionary to proactive with their giving. Over morning coffee in early December, they made a list of all the organizations they should consider giving to. The first few organizations on the list were ones who had directly impacted their lives and the lives of those they cared deeply for. It felt amazing to be able to give back to these organizations.

As they continued to work through options to give, Barb threw out an idea that stopped them both in their tracks. "Let's give it directly to people who need it." To be honest, Todd's initial reaction was not great. The banker in him came out as he recognized giving to people is not the same as giving to a 501(c)(3) organization. The result is that they would not be able to deduct those gifts for tax purposes. It just didn't make financial sense. But Barb was persistent and they decided to give it a try. They found a family who was in need during the Christmas season and helped provide a meal and gifts. This experience opened their eyes to a whole new world. While giving to people may sometimes be a little messy, it's also personal and can be so meaningful.

Todd and Barb's giving account has become one of the most enjoyable and enriching things they do within their marriage. Moving to proactive giving was a game-changer. They continue to support great organizations on a monthly basis, but it has also been amazing to witness the direct impact they can make on people through personal giving.

In time, Todd and Barb's grown kids have even started to join in. If any one of them sees a need of a friend, extended family member, or someone in their community, they send out a family text message and everyone does their best to lean in. For Todd and Barb, nothing is more beautiful than seeing their own kids catch the heart of God and live out the joy of generosity.

Exercise: Generosity

Do you wish you could give more? We all do, right? This exercise is designed to help you imagine the impact your giving could make to those organizations near to your heart. But understand, the greatest impact will be within you!

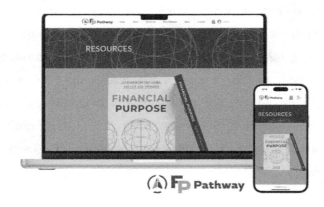

COMPLETE THE ONLINE ACTIVITY

1. Go to **https://www.fppathway.org/resources**

2. Launch the **'FP Calculator'** and complete the **Chapter 6 'Give'** section.

3. Dream big for this exercise! Don't worry about whether or not you can fund something today, add it to your list and set goals you're excited about for the future.

Discussion Questions

1. What does it mean to be a good steward of all gifts God has given us? How do your values align with God's expectation of being a steward?

2. Do you have any apprehensions about making giving your first commitment? What sacrifices do you need to make in order to achieve this?

3. What needs to happen with your spending framework to make generosity your top priority?

4. How are you letting God work within you to experience the joy of generosity?

Personal Reflection: Above All, Give Cheerfully. As you reflect on Chapter Six, what have you discovered regarding God's word about generosity? What implication will this have on how you approach your giving?

Exercise: Bring It All Together

Now it's time to bring balance to your framework. It will require you to spend time prioritizing your commitments and spending. You may need to make some short-term concessions of your goals to achieve balance today, but don't lose sight of the bigger picture. Keep your goals on the list, even if you need to reduce today's monthly commitment (even to zero). As your finances improve, update your framework to fund your future goals.

COMPLETE THE ONLINE ACTIVITY

1. Go to **https://www.fppathway.org/resources**

2. Launch the **'FP Calculator.'**
3. If you haven't done so, input your gross and net monthly income.
4. Edit each section until you have brought your framework to balance. *Hint: the 'Remaining Balance' should equal $0.00.*
5. Download or print your framework (PDF) and complete the action plan.

Exercise: Bring it All Together

COMPLETE the online activity.
Go to [link] playlist/hyperdoc here.

CHAPTER 7

Start

All hard work brings a profit,
but mere talk leads only to poverty.

Proverbs 14:23

Have you ever met a big talker?

You know the type. They're the ones who always talk about that amazing idea they have or that amazing trip they want to take. But when it comes down to it, they never actually do anything. They just talk about it.

Too often in life we fail not because we can't, but because we don't. It isn't that we can't eat healthy, we just don't make wise decisions. It isn't that we can't be a better parent, we just don't invest the energy needed. It isn't that we can't grow intellectually, we just don't take the time to read.

The same is true in our finances. The principles laid out in this book have the potential to transform every aspect of your financial life. God's wisdom gives us a blueprint for a totally new future. But these principles do nothing for you if you don't put them into action.

So... *start*.

Don't make this harder than it needs to be. Start. Will you make mistakes? Probably. But that's OK. Start anyway. Will you have to make adjustments down the road when your financial status changes? Yes. Adjustments aren't a big deal when you've already done the hard work. So, just start. Don't wait for tomorrow. Don't wait for the perfect time. Take the first step today and start. And if you get off course and trip up in your finances, it's OK. Get up, dust yourself off, and start again.

Stop talking and start. Your future self will thank you.

Action Plan: Build Your Framework

Wisdom is knowledge applied. You've done the work. You have the knowledge. Are you ready to be wise? Take the following steps to activate your framework.

☐ **Determine your commitments:**

    a.   To God (giving) $

    b.   To yourself (savings) $

    c.   To others (debt/bills) $

    d.   Set a goal or plan to be debt-free

☐ **Bring balance to your commitments and spending**

☐ **Set up your bank accounts**

☐ **Adjust your direct deposits through your payroll system**

☐ **Set up online banking for bill pay and auto transfers**

Life Applications

Introduction to Life Applications

There are moments in your financial journey that can have a disproportionate effect on your future. These moments have the potential of further fueling your financial health or they can lead you off course with devastating consequences. A little intentionality in these moments can go a long way to protecting the progress you've already made.

In this Life Applications section, we address five of the most critical financial moments in life. Although this section can be read just like any other book, it is intended to serve as a resource that you can return to and reference repeatedly in your life. We hope the information and wisdom in these pages can further help you live with *Financial Purpose*.

CHAPTER 8

Teach Your Children Well

*Start children off on the way they should go,
and even when they are old
they will not turn from it.*

Proverbs 22:6

Where did you learn about money?

In Todd's experience doing financial counseling, if you ask anyone over the age of 40, "Where did you learn about money?," the most common answer is "from my parents." But if you ask anyone under the age of 40, the answers are all over the place. It's as if several generations have forgotten to teach their kids about managing money. Is it possible this has occurred because so few of us actually know how to manage our own money well?

How we handle our money on a day-to-day basis impacts our kids' view of money, for good or for bad. If we are going to set our kids up for success in life, then being intentional about what we teach them is critical. There are three important principles to focus on when guiding your kids financially:

1. Teach your kids the foundations and fundamentals
2. Model handling money well
3. Guide them during major life events

TEACH YOUR KIDS THE FOUNDATIONS AND FUNDAMENTALS

As we've discussed throughout this book, culture's perspective on money is toxic, yet it's the dominant view. If we aren't intentional about introducing our kids to a different perspective on money (God's perspective), then the default will be for them to follow what everyone else is doing. Therefore, it is imperative to teach your kids what the Bible says about money and contrast that with culture.

God's Wisdom	Culture's Message
Spend less than you make	Spend everything and more
Save with purpose	Why save when you can borrow
Beware of debt	Borrow as much as you can
Give cheerfully	Give if there is anything left over

You've probably never thought about it, but there is no protective age limit when it comes to marketing to children. Just observe the commercials that play during cartoons. The message culture directs at your kids is simple and clear: desire more. This concise and consistent message is what inevitably leads so many people into financial bondage. Without God's wisdom to combat culture's message, most kids will never have a chance to choose a better path when it comes to money. The earlier you can begin reinforcing a biblical understanding of money, the better chance you have of setting your kids on the right trajectory. Here are a few things to consider:

HELP YOUR KIDS DEFINE FINANCIAL CATEGORIES

Two of the most basic financial categories are needs and wants. Helping your kids learn to differentiate these categories can be life-changing. Many costly financial decisions occur simply because someone has categorized a want as a need. Two other financial categories that are critical are commitments and spending. Understanding these two categories will help your kids take advantage of the financial framework we have laid out. See Chapter Three for a full explanation of these terms.

CHOOSE A BETTER PIGGY BANK

Most kids have some form of a piggy bank, but we prefer the piggy banks with three separate compartments for give, save, and live. Using this style allows for more intentionality with how your kids think about money. It reinforces the basic principle of separating your money. In addition, piggy banks like this direct kids to give and save first, then spend what is left. Small changes like this reap big dividends in your kid's financial education.

OPEN A SAVINGS ACCOUNT FIRST

When your kids are old enough to open an account at the bank, we recommend beginning with a savings account. This allows them to begin saving with purpose. As we have already discussed, we are all guilty of the "marginal propensity to spend." That means that if we have money and it doesn't have a defined purpose, we will find something to spend it on. Teach your kids how to assign purpose to every dollar they save. By determining goals to save for, it will teach them how to say no now so that they can achieve something more important later. It will also help them discover the concept of trade-offs. When every dollar in savings has a defined purpose, then when a new opportunity or desire arises, they will have to decide whether redirecting money toward that new thing is worth the trade-off.

OPEN TWO CHECKING ACCOUNTS

When the time comes to open a checking account, we recommend opening two. When your kids turn 16, have them open two checking accounts to go along with their one savings account. One checking account is for monthly commitments and one is for spending. As they earn money, deposit all of it into their savings account. Each month, auto-transfer enough money into their monthly commitments account to cover their bills and giving (granted they may not have any formal bills, but start them off right). In addition, weekly auto-transfer into their spending account to ensure they have money for their day-to-day spending. This simple and clear plan helps them establish a basic framework for managing their money that will expand as their financial life grows more complex. *It should be your goal to help each of your kids set up a complete framework prior to leaving the home.*

TEACH YOUR KIDS ABOUT DEBT, SO THEY DON'T LEARN THE HARD WAY

For many of us, we learn about debt from making our first poor decisions. The question then becomes how far in debt are we after we've made that poor decision! By teaching our kids to beware of debt, we can train them to think more critically before making life-altering decisions. Throughout their childhood, find opportunities to discuss the difference between good debt and bad debt. It's difficult to calculate a D/I ratio without steady income, but this is a great opportunity to model finances for your kids and share your D/I ratio with them. Taking the time to talk about how enslaving debt can be and how our ability to give, save, and spend is limited due to our debt payments can help inspire a life of being debt-free.

HELP YOUR KIDS UNDERSTAND WHERE TO GET THE RIGHT ADVICE

There is a difference between a trusted advisor (someone who is independent from any money transaction) and someone who gives financial advice based on a potential conflict of interest (paid commission). Who do they know that loves them and can give guidance and wisdom that is in alignment with biblical wisdom? Help them create a list of potential family members, friends, or a professional who can give them the right advice at the right time.

LANGUAGE IS IMPORTANT

As you set up your framework, take the opportunity to develop language that works for you and your family. Online banking systems allow you to nickname your accounts and we encourage you to take advantage of this. The words we have chosen throughout *Financial Purpose* are intended to create broad categories that can work for anyone. However, you may decide to use different phrases or titles that more easily resonate with you or your kids. You might prefer to title your monthly commitments category "bills." Or you might name your savings category "future goals." The key is to choose language that is easy to recite, clearly designates your categories, and provides persuasive reinforcement of the right behaviors. This becomes even more critical when communicating to your kids.

MODEL HANDLING MONEY WELL

Transparency about money can be a challenge for parents. We have a tendency to hold tightly to the privacy of our financial status. And yet, the more we can have conversations with our kids about financial matters and the more we model what healthy finances look like, the better equipped they will be for their own financial future.

Todd and Barb chose to have an open book mindset around their kids when it came to the topic of money. No question was off limits. This meant that every question became an opportunity to discuss and model how biblical principles of finance look in everyday life. By talking about how much they made, how much they paid in taxes, and how expensive it is to take care of a family, their kids were given a perspective that most kids don't receive. Each family must determine the level of candidness they will have about finances and at what age it is appropriate. A good exercise might be to include your children as you set up your own framework. If you're currently living paycheck-to-paycheck, it will be a reality check for your kids and could provide an opportunity to come together as a family to pursue financial balance.

GUIDE THEM DURING MAJOR LIFE EVENTS

Major life events are the perfect time to return to the fundamentals and take assessment of how things are going with your kids. Whether it is purchasing a new toy, a new bike, or a new car, these moments are an opportune time to reinforce the framework you have helped them establish. As they get older, these major life event moments become increasingly important to their long-term financial health.

The next four chapters outline four critical life events which impact the journey to becoming wise with money. If wise choices are made during these critical moments, a life of financial balance is achievable. But if foolish choices are made, it can lead to toxic finances that can take extreme measures to overcome. We will look at the life events of college, career, marriage and homeownership and discover the important questions we need to ask in order to chart a healthy course in our lives.

CHAPTER 9

College Bound

Teach me knowledge and good judgement,
for I trust your commands.

Psalm 119:66

There's an interesting phenomenon that exists when it comes to higher education.

The pursuit of knowledge often leads people to abandon good judgment. If you've paid any attention, you recognize that the cost of college has exploded in recent decades. But it also appears that the expectations of what the college experience should look like have also ballooned to a financially unsustainable level.

Americans currently has $1.6 trillion in student loan debt, and that number is growing. This extreme debt is leaving families and individuals with a financial burden that takes decades to pay back. Does choosing that much debt sound like using good judgment? We all believe in the pursuit of knowledge and education, but at what cost?

Dan was a proud dad and from the outside, he appeared to be a great provider. His family enjoyed a big house, expensive cars for every driver, and frequent family vacations. It appeared like they were living the American Dream. As their daughter approached her senior year of high school, Dan sought financial counsel to talk about his desire to send his daughter to a prestigious private college. The problem was, the family simply couldn't afford it. As the financial counselors assessed the family's situation, they discovered an expensive home with three mortgages, three car loans, and over $150,000 in credit card debt. Dan's American Dream was a facade riddled with poor decisions when it came to spending and debt.

The college Dan's daughter wanted to attend was estimated at over $75,000 per year. With no savings to cover it and an already massive debt load, good judgment would say to choose a less expensive option. But in the end, guess where she attended? That's right! $75,000 times four years equals $300,000 of suffocating debt. That's a pretty tough way to start your adult life. Culture won again!

In order to survive the college journey and prevent life-altering, foolish decisions, there are three principles we encourage when it comes to college:

1. Choose the right school
2. Live like a college student
3. Set a goal to be free of student loan debt

CHOOSE THE RIGHT SCHOOL

As we've encouraged, preparing for college expenses should start as early as possible. Starting a 529 savings plan for your kids when they are born is a great way to begin preparing for this significant expense. Finding ways to include your kids in the journey is also valuable as it is a great way to teach them the importance of education while also helping them understand the cost. Ultimately, you will want to set a goal for how much you want to provide for your kid's college. By doing this, you can do the simple math to figure out how much you will need to save each year to reach your goal.

As important as saving for college is, there may be nothing more important than choosing the right school. But what factors should help us determine which school is right?

Choosing the right school begins with all the normal questions: What's the location, size, student population, degrees available, etc. But the question of cost may ultimately have the biggest effect on you and your child's life.

In our section on debt, we explained how lending agencies tend to push us to borrow more money than we should. This tendency is even more exaggerated when it comes to college. It's shocking how easy it can be to borrow exorbitant amounts of money. This is why so many students leave school and struggle to get out from under the weight of their debt.

Since college expenses can be life-altering, it would make sense to take the time to analyze the potential financial impact they will have. Doing this can help you make a more informed decision that will hopefully lead to a better future. This may sound daunting, but it's actually pretty simple. Start by figuring out the yearly total cost of your college experience. Most schools can give you a reasonable estimate for this cost including all fees and books. Next, subtract the amount (if any) you or your child will be paying in cash along with any scholarships your child would receive each year. This will help you estimate how much money will need to be borrowed each year. Finally, multiply this total by the number of years your child will be enrolled in college. What you are left with is the approximate amount of debt your child will have upon graduation.

Now it's time for the rubber to meet the road. Research the average beginning salary for the career your child wants to pursue. You can use this estimated salary and go back to Fundamental One and build a financial framework using that amount. Including the monthly debt payment for college along with all other commitments and spending will allow you and your child to envision what life will look like following graduation. Will they have enough money to live? Will they struggle to get by? Is that level of debt sustainable? You can also use these numbers to estimate your child's debt-to-income ratio to further understand what their financial position will look like following college.

By taking the time to think through the full consequences of your college selection, you will be able to make a more informed decision. But as with all decisions, it's yours to make. However, taking a little extra time before you decide can save you and your child years of financial pain later in life.

Make the wise decision. Choose the *right* school.

LIVE LIKE A COLLEGE STUDENT

As you walk through the journey of selecting a school, you'll be amazed how each child will look at college campuses through a different lens. Some will be most interested in academics, others the sports, others the location, and still others the prestige of the school. Your child's personality will play a part in finding the right school they want to attend.

However, you must be aware how hard universities work to sell the "college experience" to attract new students. Whether it's the investments they've made in new buildings, commitment to athletic facilities, upscale food options, or the many activities available on campus, colleges work hard to compete for new enrollment. But all of these enhancements come at a cost, and that cost is passed on to the student.

Some universities have even upgraded their dormitories to feel more like luxury condominiums. These extravagantly adorned facilities boast fabulous amenities, but they come with a hefty price tag. All the while, these schools will advertise that these upgraded facilities can be paid for with student loans.

Hear this:

If you have to borrow money to live like a king or queen in college, chances are you'll live like a peasant the rest of your life!

It's far better to make the wise choice by learning to live like a college student. Limiting expenses during the college years can eliminate years of additional debt payments. Find ways to save money. Work a part-time job. Eat mac and cheese sometimes. By avoiding the temptation to live extravagantly in college, you can pave the way to a financially healthier life for years to come.

SET A GOAL TO BE FREE OF STUDENT LOAN DEBT

It's simple. The less you spend while attending school, the less debt you'll have. The less debt you have, the quicker you'll be able to pay it off. And the quicker you pay off your loans, the quicker you can start living the life God wants you to live! Here are some tips for paying off your loans fast:

- If interest is charged on your loans while you're still in school (and most are), pay the interest as you go. Most student loans allow you to delay paying the interest until after graduation, but the lender simply adds that interest to the loan. The result is that you end up paying interest on the interest (compounding interest) and this will cost you more money in the future.

- As we described in Chapter Five, use the snowball method to pay off your loans. Snowballing debt works.

- If you desire to consolidate student loans following college, be careful about who you borrow from. Most lenders want you to refinance all of your loans into one and then stretch the payments out as long as possible. This means they collect more interest for a longer period. In the end, it can cost you tens of thousands of dollars in extra payments. There are so many bad practices when it comes to refinancing student loans. Therefore, it's important to find an advisor who is trustworthy and has your best interests in mind. At a minimum, pick a lender who: (1) Recommends no additional cash advances; (2) Encourages you to choose the shortest loan term you can afford; and (3) Offers a competitive fixed rate option to lock in your payments until it's paid.

Your child's education can be one of the most impactful elements to their adult life, for good or for bad. Taking the time to support them in using good judgment can make all the difference!

CHAPTER 10

Your First Day of Your First Job

*Commit your work to the Lord,
and your plans will be established.*

Proverbs 16:3 ESV

Most people show up to their first day of work unprepared.

And no, I'm not talking about the fact that they are unprepared for their new job. That's normal. No one expects you to be fully trained and ready to be proficient and productive on the first day. It can take months for that to happen.

However, when you arrive at work on the first day, something takes place that you probably haven't even thought about. As you're welcomed into your new place of employment, much of the first day is spent with Human Resources. You often receive training on the important policies, guidelines, and culture of the organization. But somewhere along the line, you'll be asked a number of questions that will impact the course of your financial journey for the rest of your life. In order to answer wisely, be prepared with the following disciplines:

1. Maximize your benefits on DAY ONE
2. Get your tax withholding (W4) right
3. Reset Fundamental One: Spend Less Than You Make

MAXIMIZE YOUR BENEFITS ON *DAY ONE*

Many employment opportunities include benefits that are available to the employees. These benefits are in addition to the base salary and can provide options that must be considered wisely. There are many forms that benefits can take, but three of the most common are health insurance, life and disability insurance, and retirement. Each of these opportunities can have a substantial effect on your present and future life. It's therefore critical to make decisions thoughtfully and deliberately.

HEALTH INSURANCE

Medical and dental insurance are two options that are often available as a benefit of employment. Each employer customizes their own plan and it is important for you to know what is available to you. Before deciding, make sure to read all materials provided so that you can make the decision that is best for you and your current situation. Making the right choice upfront will pay dividends for you in the long run. Often there are tools that help guide you through the process of choosing the plan that best fits your needs. Take advantage of these tools as they can help you forecast what your needs will be. Remember: Insurance enrollments are done annually, which means you can make adjustments each year based on what is best for you and your family.

Many companies encourage high deductible plans for medical insurance. Generally, if you're in good health, this can be a good path to choose. The premiums are typically lower as much of the front end of medical expenses are transferred to you through the higher deductible. This means you save money if you infrequently use medical services. The hidden benefit of a high deductible plan is the eligibility of a Health Saving Account (HSA). An HSA is a great vehicle to build savings for future medical expenses. If done properly, the money is typically invested on a pre-tax basis so you do not pay state or federal income tax on the amount contributed. Withdrawals are tax-free for qualifying medical expenses. Many employers encourage engagement by making or matching contributions. Each year, the IRS sets contribution limits for HSAs. By challenging yourself to reach the maximum contribution each year, an HSA gives you the ability to accumulate a significant asset over a lifetime.

LIFE AND DISABILITY INSURANCE

None of us plan on being unable to work, but we can all prepare for the possibility. To help you deal with unfortunate circumstances, many employers offer options for these two types of insurance. It's important to understand what is available to you and to take full advantage of these benefits.

However, the challenge is trying to figure out how much coverage is needed for you and any dependents you have. Making things even more difficult is the fact that the amount of coverage you need will often require a combination of employer provided insurance as well as insurance purchased outside of work.

Why do you need to consider insurance outside of your employer's plan? Insurance purchased through your employer is not permanent. If you lose or quit your job, the insurance will end. Medical issues or injuries can lead to job loss, so it is important to have a base of both life and disability insurance while you are still insurable. In addition, employer provided insurance may not be enough to meet your financial needs. There are usually limits on life and disability benefits. This limit may create a gap between your income and your expenses when you need it the most. Expenses will often increase during life or disability claim periods.

Most insurances outside of work are priced based on insurability. When you are young or in good health, premiums are at their lowest. It's best to take advantage of this time to purchase the right products at the lowest cost. However, one of the benefits of employer sponsored plans is that they are typically guaranteed to be issued. If insurability is a barrier for you, taking full advantage of your employer sponsored options could be what is best.

Finally, determining the amount of insurance you need is not magic. It's a formula based on your individual situation and needs. A good financial advisor can assist you in determining how much insurance you will need as well as help you find the proper balance of employer and non-employer provided insurance. And just like health insurance, this is something that can be adjusted regularly as your life circumstances and needs change.

RETIREMENT

Retirement may not be on your mind the first day of your first job. However, it's important to realize the decisions you make on day one to begin preparing for retirement will ultimately determine your future path. No decision is a decision! Too many people delay contributing to things like a 401k with the hope of dealing with it later in life. In the meantime, they build a lifestyle based on their current paycheck. Unfortunately, when you've become accustomed to a certain level of income, it can be very difficult to unwind that lifestyle to begin contributing to retirement accounts. Beginning to save on day one is the easiest way to ensure you set a course for long-term financial health.

A typical employer will match dollar for dollar up to 6% of your income for a 401k. As a result, the average contribution rate for people under 40 is between 7-8%. It's crazy not to make sure you contribute enough to receive the company match. You are literally missing out on free money. But if you want to retire at or before 65, this is not enough. At a minimum, it is recommended that you invest between 10% to 15% of your income for retirement.

In addition to these primary benefits offered by employers, look for other benefits available in your specific circumstance. Some companies offer benefits related to childcare expenses, student loan repayment, and even ongoing education. Certain companies also offer profit sharing and stock options. As Todd and Barb's son, Eric, launched his career, the three of them reviewed his benefits package. It was filled with nuggets for saving money, which have proven to be a real windfall. The company he joined is an Employee Stock Ownership Plan (ESOP). In addition to the 401k benefit, profit sharing and stock options were also available. Within just a few years, Eric has developed a balanced portfolio and is on a path to financial success. **Take advantage of what your employer wants to give you.** By leveraging all of these opportunities, you can make the most of your situation and set yourself up for the healthiest financial future possible.

GET YOUR TAX WITHHOLDING (W4) RIGHT

Let's be honest, nobody likes talking about taxes. Yet it's a reality we all must deal with. Taking the time to make the right decisions on day one will benefit you all year long.

Both the federal and state governments withhold money from your paycheck for taxes. The amount that is withheld is an estimate of your taxes for a calendar year. Your goal is to select the right amount of money to be withheld so that it covers your actual taxes, not too much and not too little. If you don't withhold enough, you will be left paying additional taxes at the end of the year and potentially even paying a penalty and interest. If you withhold too much, you will receive a refund at the end of the year, but you ended up giving the government an interest-free loan for the year.

Everyone's tax situation is unique. To determine the amount of taxes to withhold from your paycheck, you will fill out an IRS form called a W4. The form comes with a set of instructions and a worksheet to help you determine the number of exemptions you may file. The more exemptions you have, the fewer taxes are withheld. It is helpful to get a copy of the W4 and instructions before your first day of work (these can be found online at www.irs.gov). This will give you the opportunity to review the form, research any questions you might have, and complete the worksheet.

Taxes are a mystery to the average person and without a history of employment the first year is almost a complete unknown. But most people set it (W4) and forget it. However, you can change your W4 at any time. Remember, the goal is the choose the right amount. If at any time in the year you complete an estimate of your taxes and you see that you'll be above or below your goal, you can fill out a new W4 and make the appropriate adjustment. As you complete your taxes at the end of each year, look at the results of your withholding. If you're paying additional taxes or receiving a larger refund, go ahead and make the needed adjustments to your W4.

RESET FUNDAMENTAL ONE: SPEND LESS THAN YOU MAKE

Once you've received your first paycheck, it's time to return to Fundamental One. Take the time to reset your financial framework by accounting for your new income. This includes assessing new commitments in the areas of giving and saving. It may also include commitments such as rent, utilities, loan payments, and insurance. Similarly, it's necessary to account for the spending that may be necessary in this new season of life. By establishing an updated framework, you are able to ensure you maintain healthy finances. And if another adjustment happens in the future, it's time for another reset.

Here's the key: If you take the time to honor your commitments first, including items like your benefits, taxes, and retirement funding, then you will build a lifestyle with what remains. And this is what it means to live with *Financial Purpose*. It means living in the blessing and freedom that flows from following God's wisdom for our money.

CHAPTER 11

Marriage

And the two will become one flesh...

Mark 10:8a

Todd and Barb's daughter, Micayla, and her fiancé, Jared, were a month out from their wedding day.

Like many couples, they were enrolled in a premarital course with nine other couples. On this day, the group leader entered the room with a simple yet startling statement, "This week we're going to talk about money." The topic seemed obvious for a premarital course, but his first question brought the room to a standstill: "Have you talked about how you're going to handle your money after you're married?" The awkward silence said it all. It was obvious that most of the couples were yet to deal with this critical question.

Money is emotional and has been the cause of countless marital arguments and divorces. Yet, most couples who walk down the aisle never take the time to talk about how they are going to manage their money together. This is not only foolish, but it can be painful. To make handling your money a strength in your marriage, implement the following principles:

1. Agree on ground rules
2. Develop a joint framework
3. Communicate, communicate, communicate

AGREE ON GROUND RULES

Ground rules are critical to set the culture and tone for how you are going to handle money in your marriage. Why? Because we all come into marriage with our own set of knowledge and experiences. We have different parents or guardians who taught us different values. We have different siblings or friends who influence our behavior. We grew up in different neighborhoods, communities, and churches. And beyond that, we all have our own unique personalities and preferences. So, it's not surprising that our views of money can often be quite different as we come together in marriage. The best way to start down a healthy path is to agree on ground rules. The list of ground rules doesn't need to be lengthy or complex, but you both need to fully buy in and commit to them. Here are three rules we highly recommend:

WE ARE ONE

This means that all income is now *our* income. There's no mine and yours, but only ours. This change in mindset can be difficult at first, but it is the greatest way to ensure that you have a shared vision for your financial future. All income goes into the family framework where it is then allocated based on your mutual priorities. Individual needs and wants can still be accounted for by making intentional decisions together while planning.

WE ARE A TEAM

Money cannot be the responsibility of only one person in a marriage. Both partners need to be engaged and invested in the management of money. You may choose different roles based on each person's gifts, but both of you need to be involved. Without this, management of the money will create ongoing frustration in your home. One person will feel in the dark about where the money goes and the other will feel like the budget police. Choosing to work together will make for better finances and a better marriage.

WE ARE TRANSPARENT

When we lack transparency, trust is in danger. Choosing to be totally honest and open about your money situation will lead to a healthier financial future and relationship. Before you get married, it's important to be honest about things like income and debt. As time goes on, items like taxes, retirement savings, investments, and insurances should be discussed openly. Withholding information like this from one another will only lead to a toxic outcome.

These three rules form a strong foundation for how any couple should relate to their money together. From here, you can add your own rules that make sense for your relationship. Some examples could include separate personal accounts, dollar limits on spending without the agreement of the other spouse, or even what gets cut first if you come up short during the month. Having a few rules in place ahead of time makes decisions easier and ensures you stay unified.

DEVELOP A JOINT FRAMEWORK

"And the two will become one flesh," (Mark 10:8a) isn't just a cute Scripture to have inscribed on a wedding picture frame. This should be the pursuit of every marriage, even when it comes to finances. To accomplish this, we challenge every married couple to have one framework for all your money. This means one account for monthly commitments, one account for non-monthly commitments, one spending account, and one savings account.

Couples who choose to have divided accounts unnecessarily turn every purchase into a battle over whose turn it is to pay. Whether it's the mortgage, a movie, or a meal, each purchase requires a decision about who will fund it. By establishing one framework, it eliminates unnecessary conflict and produces simplified finances.

COMMUNICATE, COMMUNICATE, COMMUNICATE

Have you ever heard that healthy communication is key to marriage? It's true.

Unfortunately, most couples struggle in this area. And it only gets more difficult when it comes to finances. Money conversations are usually charged with emotion because either too much is being spent, not enough money has been saved, or the burden of debt is weighing heavy. And because it's uncomfortable to talk about money, it's often only dealt with when things get really bad.

By working together to develop a framework for your marriage, you will begin a healthier journey of communicating about money. Working through the process of building your own framework will enable you to discuss your values, priorities, and future dreams. Being honest about things like generosity, family vacations, and retirement gives you the chance to understand each other at a deeper level and ensure that you develop a pathway to reach those desires.

But once you've established a framework, the communicating *cannot* stop! It is critical to normalize discussing your finances and making decisions together. The more your financial decisions are made together, the less opportunity there is to allow money to become a source of division in your home.

Since all your commitments are dealt with in your framework, the most important place to stay in communication about is your spending. You can decide the rhythm that works best for you, but establishing a habit of regularly connecting on your spending will help make certain your finances are moving the right direction. It is also helpful to set aside time each year to re-evaluate your goals and dreams. It will help you make decisions for your framework and remain unified with a common vision for the future.

Micayla and Jared's premarital class didn't end with an uncomfortable financial question. In fact, the question was just the beginning. Micayla and Jared had already taken the time to establish their own framework for their marriage and were fully prepared for this new season of life. Instead of staying silent, Micayla began to share with the group about how this system of organizing money had allowed them to feel confident about their future together. After clearly laying out their framework, the overwhelming question from the group was, "How do *we* do that?" In response, Micayla recruited her brother, Chris, a certified financial planner. Chris strongly believes in the framework, both on a professional and personal level. He incorporates this framework into the financial foundation for the clients he works with. The two of them set up a workshop for the entire group to walk through the process of building their own framework. Ultimately, they were able to help nine other couples begin their financial story in a healthy way.

CHAPTER 12

First-Time Homeownership

By wisdom a house is built,
and through understanding it is established...

Proverbs 24:3

This might surprise you, but the biggest risk to your long-term financial security is overbuying a home.

Homeownership is a beautiful thing. More than simply a place to live, a home can be a source of blessings for you and your family for generations. Beyond that, there may be nothing that makes you feel more grown up than buying your first home. However, careless decisions during the home buying process can strap you with unmanageable debt and prevent you from ever reaching the dreams you have for your life.

Why is the home buying process so dangerous? Well, the entire industry is set up for you to overbuy. More specifically, the industry is set up for you to buy the biggest and most expensive home *they* say you can afford (see Chapter Five for discussion of debt-to-income ratio). During the buying process, most people work with two advisors: A realtor and a mortgage loan officer (MLO). Both of these advisors are paid based on how much home you buy. Their income goes up when you spend more money. This is clearly a conflict of interest and helps explain why so many people find themselves being house poor (having an expensive home that prevents you from living the life you really want). The best thing to do when contemplating purchasing a home is to surround yourself with advisors who are looking out for your long-term, best interests. Good financial advisors can help you see the big picture and understand the unseen trade-offs that purchasing an expensive home require. To set yourself up for successful homeownership, follow these principles:

1. Dream in reality
2. Buy wisely
3. Take care of your investment

DREAM IN REALITY

A typical home buying process looks something like this: You begin by dreaming about the home you want by searching online and watching TV shows for inspiration. Once you have a feel for what you want, you find a realtor to show you some options. Often, the first question the realtor asks is, "Are you pre-approved for a home loan?" If you haven't already done so, you decide to connect with a MLO. The natural question most people want to ask is, "How much can I spend?" (This is the wrong question, but we will come back to this.) The MLO does some quick calculations and gives you the maximum amount of money you can spend on a home. In just a few minutes time, you walk out of their door with a pre-approval letter authorizing you to purchase a home for that maximum amount.

From this point on, you've all but guaranteed you'll spend more money than you can afford. Why? Because, as we discussed in Chapter Five, the MLO follows the guidelines set by the mortgage industry and qualifies your purchase based on a simple D/I ratio. Currently that amount is set at 43% of your gross income. That percentage is unsustainable for nearly everyone. Having an MLO approve that level of debt is different than you sitting down and determining how much you can actually afford to pay on a monthly basis. But because you now have a letter of approval, it begins to plant the idea in your mind that you can afford that much. It's easy to want to trust the approval letter of the MLO because they're experts. Besides, everyone else appears to be able to afford nice homes, so you convince yourself that you will find a way to make it work too.

You head back to your realtor with a pre-approval letter and they begin to schedule appointments to see homes for the maximum amount possible. And as they say, the rest is history. You have set yourself up to spend far more money than you can practically afford. And the difficulty is that this becomes a long-term decision. Most homes are purchased with a 30-year mortgage. This means that for most of your adult life, you will be strapped with a mortgage payment that you can't really afford.

So... what's the answer?

Rather than beginning by dreaming of the home you want and hoping you can afford it, dream in reality. Begin with your framework. Take an honest look at your financial situation and determine how much you can afford to pay. This includes adding together your mortgage payment (principle, interest, taxes, and insurance), new utility costs, and any changes in your commuting expenses (gas, bus...). In addition, it's an industry standard that you set aside 1-2% of your home's value each year to pay for maintenance and upkeep. By adding this together, you can determine how much home you *SHOULD* buy rather than how much you *COULD* buy.

Now that you have an amount set that is both allowable by the bank and sustainable by you, you can begin to look for homes. Taking this time will enable you to make a purchase that will bless your life rather than suffocate you.

BUY WISELY

For most people, buying a home is the biggest purchase they ever make. Because of this, it's important to engage more than our emotions in order to make the right decisions. There are a few moments in the buying process when it is critical to buy wisely.

When choosing a lender, many people only think about the interest rate of the loan. Although this is very important, it is also critical to understand the fees associated with the loan. Lenders can offer lower rates, but make up for it in the fees they charge. A good lender will take the time to fully explain how their rates and fees work. Also, a good lender will help you answer the question, "How much *should* I spend?" instead of, "How much *can* I spend?" If they are pushing you to spend beyond what you can afford, then find a new lender! Also, understand that interest rates are constantly moving up and down based on market conditions. It's like stock values or the price of gas. A good lender will help you know when the right time is to lock in your interest rate.

Considering the condition of the home is both of practical and financial importance. After you have had an inspection of the home, determine if there are any issues that need to be dealt with and which of these issues will be taken care of by the seller. Any items not dealt with by the seller will become your responsibility. Repairs, appliances that need replacing, or worn-out flooring are just some of the items that can carry significant expenses. By understanding the needs of the home and the associated costs, you can better understand how much this new home will really cost you.

Furnishing a home is often forgotten during the initial purchase process. Once you own that home, you have to fill it. Whether it's beds, couches, shower curtains, rugs, or any other home items, furnishing a home can be very expensive and should be thought about prior to purchasing. Some people will intentionally determine to leave a room empty until they have the money to fill it. Others may decide to downsize to ensure that they can afford to fully furnish their home. The decision is yours, but should be thought through prior to making a purchase.

When it comes to your mortgage, pick the shortest term you can afford. Most people pick a 30-year mortgage regardless of their situation. Although 30 years might be reasonable for a first-time home buyer, as you get older and want to upgrade your home it may be better to choose a shorter term. Always consider your future goals. When do you plan on retiring? When do you want to be debt-free? Knowing this can help you make the best decision for your future.

TAKE CARE OF YOUR INVESTMENT

If you're going to spend hundreds of thousands of dollars on an investment, it only makes sense to do everything you can to keep your home in good shape. The long-term value of your home depends on it!

Take time to think through all the current and future needs of your home and plan accordingly. This means thinking about routine maintenance items, general updating costs, and preparing for unexpected repairs. In addition, planning ahead for large replacement costs such as roofs or furnaces can ensure you are prepared when those needs arise. As mentioned, the industry standard is to set aside 1-2% of the value of your home each year for maintenance and upkeep of your home. Once you have considered all these needs, make sure to include these items in your framework under the proper category (monthly commitments, non-monthly commitments, or savings).

Owning a home is a desire for most people. By taking the time to make wise and thoughtful decisions, you can ensure that your home is a blessing and not a burden for years to come.

For where your treasure is, there your heart will be also.

Matthew 6:21

Closing Prayer

Lord, we know that the things we treasure ultimately capture our heart. Above everything else in this world, we ask that you would help us treasure you and your wisdom. Teach us to walk in your ways and live in your freedom so that we can honor you all the days of our lives.

Amen

Endnotes

[1] Huddleston, Cameron. "Survey: 69% of Americans Have Less Than $1,000 in Savings." *Yahoo.com*, 16 December 2019, https://finance.yahoo.com/news/survey-69-americans-less-1-171927256.html

[2] Manning-Schaffer, Vivian. "Most of Us Live Paycheck-to-Paycheck. This Is What It Does to Your Health." *NBCnews*, 2 November 2017, https://www.nbcnews.com/better/health/most-us-live-paycheck-paycheck-what-itdoes-your-health-ncna816411

[3] Huddleston, Cameron. "Survey: 69% of Americans Have Less Than $1,000 in Savings." *Yahoo.com*, 16 December 2019, https://finance.yahoo.com/news/survey-69-americans-less-1-171927256.html

[4] Connell, Shaun. "Debt Stats: 'What Percentage of American Citizens Are In Debt?'" *Credit Building Tips*, 3 December 2022, https://creditbuildingtips.com/percentage-american-citizens-debt/

[4] Tappe, Anneken. "Americans have never been in so much debt." 11 November 2021, *CNN Business*, https://www.cnn.com/2021/11/09/economy/fed-household-debt-inflation/index.html

[5] Stefan, Melissa. "AN INSIDE LOOK AT CHURCH ATTENDERS WHO TITHE THE MOST." 17 May 2013, *Christianity Today*, https://www.christianitytoday.com/news/2013/may/inside-look-at-church-attenders-who-tithe-most.html

[6] White, Alexandria. "Nearly 75% of All Americans Rank Money as the #1 Stress in Life." 20 May 2024, *CNBC*, https://www.cnbc.com/select/73-percent-of-americans-rank-finances-as-the-number-one-stress-in-life/

[7] Varu, Vaishali. "The Real Reason Couples Argue About Money." 11 May 2023, *Kiplinger*, https://www.kiplinger.com/personal-finance/spending/the-real-reasons-couples-argue-about-money

[8] DiGangi, Christine. "Americans are dying with an average of $62k of debt." 25 March 2017, *ABC News*, https://abcnews.go.com/Business/americans-dying-average-62k-debt/story?id=46323519

[9] Dodd, Brian, "Generous Church: Ten Top Characteristics." 10 September 2022, *CHURCHLEADERS*, https://churchleaders.com/pastors/pastor-how-to/151049-brian-dodd-generous-church-ten-top-characteristics.html

[10] Hurd, Erin, "Does Using a Credit Card Make You Spend More Money?" 28 May 2024, *Nerdwallet*, https://www.nerdwallet.com/article/credit-cards/credit-cards-make-you-spend-more

[10] Greene, Claire and Schuh, Scott. "The 2016 Diary of Consumer Payment Choice." 1 December 2017, *Federal Reserve, Bank of Boston*, https://www.bostonfed.org/publications/research-data-report/2017/the-2016-diary-of-consumer-payment-choice.aspx

[10] Peterson, Bailey, "Credit Card Spending Studies: Why You Spend More When You Pay With a Credit Card." 22 March 2018, *ValuePenguin*, https://www.valuepenguin.com/credit-cards/credit-card-spending-studies

[11] "THE AMERICAN MIDDLE CLASS IS LOSING GROUND." 9 December 2015, *Pew Research Center*, https://www.pewresearch.org/social-trends/2015/12/09/acknowledgments/

Made in the USA
Monee, IL
01 April 2025

14827726R00089